RACHMANINOFF

FANTAISIE-TABLEAUX
(SUITE NO. 1)

OP. 5
FOR TWO PIANOS, FOUR HANDS

EDITED BY MAURICE HINSON AND ALLISON NELSON

AN ALFRED MASTERWORK EDITION

Copyright © 2018 by Alfred Music
All rights reserved.   Printed in USA.
ISBN-10: 1-4706-3965-3
ISBN-13: 978-1-4706-3965-5

Cover art: The Dance *(date unknown)*
By Filipp Malyavin (Russian, 1869–1940)
Oil on canvas

SERGEI RACHMANINOFF

Contents

Sergei Rachmaninoff

FANTAISIE-TABLEAUX (Suite No. 1), Op. 5

Edited by Maurice Hinson and Allison Nelson

ABOUT THE COMPOSER

Foreword

Sergei Rachmaninoff was born in Oneg, Russia on April 1, 1873, and died in Beverly Hills, California on March 28, 1943. He studied at both the St. Petersburg and Moscow conservatories with the teachers Anton Arensky (1861–1906), Sergei Taneyev (1856–1915), and his cousin Alexander Siloti (1863–1945).

As with many great composers, Rachmaninoff's ability was recognized in his late teens. He wrote his *Piano Concerto No. 1*, Op. 1, in 1890–91 (and later revised it in 1917). At the age of 19, he signed a contract with the Russian publishing firm Gutheil. Shortly after signing the contract, he composed *Morceaux de fantaisie*, Op. 3, a collection of five pieces that includes the famous "Prelude in C-sharp Minor." The *Fantaisie-tableaux (Suite No. 1)*, Op. 5, for two pianos followed in 1893.

In addition to composing, Rachmaninoff became the second conductor of the Moscow Private Russian Opera Company in 1897, a position in which he gained a thorough knowledge of both Russian and European opera. His first professional travels outside of Russia in the spring of 1899 took him to London, where he conducted his symphonic poem *The Rock*, Op. 7, and performed selections of solo piano works.

Rachmaninoff in 1915

Rachmaninoff's *Symphony No. 1*, Op. 13, premiered in St. Petersburg on March 27, 1897, within a week of the composer's 24th birthday. The orchestra was conducted by composer and later director of the St. Petersburg Conservatory Alexander Glazunov (1865–1936). The reviews were disastrous. As a result of the searing criticism, Rachmaninoff succumbed to a mental breakdown that lasted for three years, during which time he lost his inspiration for composing. After treatment by the psychologist Nikolai Dahl (1860–1939), Rachmaninoff recovered and began composing again. This period of creativity is notable for some of his most lasting masterworks. Between 1900 and 1903, he produced the *Suite No. 2* (for two pianos), Op. 17 (composed 1900–01); the famous *Piano Concerto No. 2*, Op. 18 (1900–01); the *Cello Sonata*, Op. 19 (1901); the *Variations on a Theme of Chopin*, Op. 22 (1903); and the *Ten Preludes*, Op. 23 (1901–03). These works contain some similarities, including nostalgically Romantic writing and long, lyrical melodies.

Rachmaninoff continued to pursue his career in conducting, which took him to Moscow and London. He also conducted at the Bolshoi Theater from 1904 to 1906. In 1906, he composed his incomparable *Symphony No. 2*, Op. 27, a work of magnificent melodies and soaring climaxes. By this time, his compositional Romantic style was fully developed, although he would continue to experiment with new harmonic and rhythmic ideas. Throughout his life, he despised what was being called "modern music."

Rachmaninoff's piano music, written in an eclectic individual style, derives from the Romantic pianism of Chopin, Liszt, Schumann, Tchaikovsky, and Brahms, but it is also flavored with Russian sounds. Rachmaninoff's melodic writing is of the highest order and is supported by sonorous harmonies with florid decorations, resulting in highly effective music for the piano. Although Rachmaninoff composed operas, orchestral works, choral music, chamber music, and songs, his piano works, more than anything else, have made him world famous.

Rachmaninoff first visited the United States in 1909, when he premiered his *Piano Concerto No. 3*, Op. 30, in New York. He returned to Russia and continued living there, conducting a number of Moscow Philharmonic concerts during the 1912–1913 season. He left Russia permanently in 1917 when the Communist Revolution took place. Rachmaninoff returned to the United States, where he developed an international career as a concert pianist and, over time, produced an extensive collection of recordings. He became one of the most revered pianists of the 20th century.

In 1926, Rachmaninoff completed his *Piano Concerto No. 4*, Op. 40, which he had begun in 1914. In 1934, he composed one of his finest works for piano and orchestra, the *Rhapsody on a Theme of Paganini*, Op. 43. This work was followed in 1936 by his *Symphony No. 3*, Op. 44. His last trip to London was in 1938, and in 1939 he performed his final piano recital in that city.

"Rachmaninoff: The Last Concert" by Russian sculptor Victor Bokarov.

Rachmaninoff's sculpture and plaque in the World's Fair Park in Knoxville, Tennessee.

Photo by David Loebbaka

Rachmaninoff embarked on a concert tour of the United States in 1942. On November 9 of that year, he cancelled a recital in Knoxville, Tennessee, due to illness. On February 15, 1943, although he was seriously ill at the time, he fulfilled his obligation and performed the last concert of his career in Knoxville. A few weeks later, he died in his Beverly Hills home, shortly after he and his wife received their American citizenship.

ABOUT THE MUSIC

Rachmaninoff spent the summer of 1893 at the Lysikofs' Estate outside of Kharkov. From there he wrote: "At the present time I am working on a *Fantasy* for two pianos, consisting of musical pictures."[1] This is the work now known as *Suite No. 1*, Op. 5. It was first performed in Moscow on November 30, 1893 by Rachmaninoff and Pavel Pabst (1854–1897). Pabst was a professor at the Moscow Conservatory and a well-known pianist and teacher.

This large work demands exceptional technique and Romantic expression from both pianists. This is one of the very few works that sound as if two pianos were the only possible medium for the music. The suite also displays Rachmaninoff's virtuosity as a pianist. Many pyrotechnical figurations and numerous rippling arpeggios demonstrate that the music could only have been composed by a superb pianist.

Rachmaninoff's theory about performing keyboard music applies to this work.

> Each piece has a culminating point. The culmination. . .may be at the end or in the middle, it may be loud or soft, but the performer must know how to approach it with absolute calculation, absolute precision, because if it slips by then the whole construction crumbles, then the whole piece becomes disjointed and scrappy and does not convey to the listener what must be conveyed.[2]

This four-movement work is dedicated to Peter Ilyich Tchaikovsky (1840–1893), who was a great admirer of Rachmaninoff. Tchaikovsky had planned to attend the premier but died a few weeks prior to it and consequently was never able to hear the piece. In the first edition, each movement is prefaced by a few lines of poetry. The first, third, and fourth movements are preceded by poems of the Russian authors Mikhail Lermontov, Fyodor Tyoutchev, and Aleksey Khomiakov. The poem before the second movement is by English poet Lord Byron. In this edition, the Russian poems have been translated by Natalia Matskevich-Levin.

Rachmaninoff in 1921

1   Barrie Martyn, *Rachmaninoff: Composer, Pianist, Conductor* (Hants, England: Scholar Press, 1990), 75.
2   Geoffrey Norris, "Rakhmaninov, Sergey" in *The New Grove Dictionary of Music and Musicians*, ed. Stanley Sadie, Vol. 15 (London: Macmillan Publishers Limited, 1980), 555.

The musical term *barcarolle* comes from the Italian word *barca*, meaning boat. It is a composition, usually in $\frac{6}{8}$ time, that imitates the lilting boat songs of gondoliers. This movement, in G minor, has the typical swaying feel of other barcarolles but is in $\frac{3}{4}$ time. The main theme appears in Piano I between measures 4 and 12 and is followed by florid and highly ornamented repetitions of the melody. In G major at measure 90, Piano I is instructed to play *la melodia marcato*. This means to bring out the large notes (the melody) while playing the smaller accompanying notes softly through measure 120. Similar sections occur between measures 132 (*cantabile*) and 160, and in G minor between measures 194 (*un poco meno mosso*) and 214. Colorful arabesques and arpeggios spin around the themes, reflecting the lapping waves described in the accompanying poem.

The poem that precedes the movement is by Mikhail Yuryevich Lermontov (1814–1841), a Russian writer and painter from the Romantic period. In addition to being a poet, he was also influential as a novelist.

Form (**ABCBACA Coda**):

Introduction = mm. 1–4
A = 4–67
B = 67–90
C = 90–120
B = 120–160
A = 160–194
C = 194–213
A = 214–231
Coda = 231–250

This movement is related to the subject material of the first movement with a continuing theme of love and colorful, passionate writing. The entire range of the keyboard is explored with a constant dialogue between the parts. The peaceful mood shifts between major and minor harmonies, and the textures are filled extensively with shimmering trills, arpeggios, and tremolos.

In measures 1 through 16, the opening theme in Piano II suggests a trumpet or horn signaling the hour (a total of nine "chimes"). Measure 18 introduces a high repeated C-natural, which is the beginning of a nightingale's melody, characterized by trills, grace notes, and capricious rhythms.

Measure 30 marks the beginning of the **B** section. Here a softer dynamic is accompanied by a change of texture. Oscillating intervals in Piano I suggest swirling waters, while an *amoroso* melody in Piano II might represent the declarative vows of two young lovers. The nightingale melody returns in measure 32 of Piano I. A flourish of 32nd-note arpeggios emerges in Piano II at measure 36, creating an antagonistic backdrop while the lovers' amorous melody continues, now in octaves, in Piano I. The water motive reappears in Piano I in measure 43, accompanying a restatement of the trumpet theme in Piano I. This duet continues to the *fff* climax of the movement at measure 59. The wind, water, trumpet, and nightingale motives are interwoven from measure 60 to the end of the movement, where after a long diminuendo both pianos finish with *pp* chords. In measures 129–130, the last three notes in the upper voice of Piano II echo the opening theme.

The poem that precedes the movement is by George Gordon Byron (1788–1824), who is usually known as Lord Byron. An Englishman, he is considered one of the most important poets of the Romantic period. The excerpt that accompanies this movement is from his poem *Parisina*.

Form (**ABCD Coda**):

A = 1–29
B = 30–42
C = 43–60
D = 60–124

Coda = 124–130

III. Les larmes (Tears)

The final two movements of the suite both feature the sound of bells. The third movement was inspired by the bells of St. Sofia's Cathedral in Novgorod, which Rachmaninoff visited with his grandmother Butabova when he was a youngster. In this movement, Rachmaninoff associates the sound of the bells with sadness.

A four-note descending motive is heard throughout (91 times) in many variations that display versatile pianistic invention. The overall effect of the work is one of deep agony and despair, culminating in a coda reminiscent of a funeral march, beginning at measure 47. The last statement of the opening theme is in measures 54 and 55 of Piano I.

The poem that precedes this movement is by Fyodor Ivanovich Tyutchev (1803–1873), a Russian poet of the Romantic period. He was known for his liberal views, but his poetry on political subjects is mainly forgotten.

Form: through-composed, with **Coda**

Sergei Rachmaninoff (ca. 1920)

This final movement captures the sound of Russian church-bell ringers. German composer and musicologist Oskar Riesemann was a long-time acquaintance of Rachmaninoff and published a biography of the composer in 1934, based on conversations he had with Rachmaninoff in 1930. He describes this finale as follows:

> The last movement contains a wonderful carillon—the first Rachmaninoff ever composed— which resembles the fanatic peal of Orthodox Church bells on Easter Sunday as closely as can be managed with the tones of the piano. We know that Rachmaninoff since his earliest childhood had shown the greatest interest in the musical side of the Russian Church ritual. Like many other Russian composers he was fascinated by the task of reproducing the 'irrational' sound of a Russian peal and the wonderful rhythmic intricacies produced by the practiced hands of the ringers, on ordinary musical instruments, with the aid of measurable notes.[3]

This movement is the shortest of the four. It opens with brilliant figuration in Piano I before the bells begin to toll in Piano II at measure 3. The mood is celebratory and jubilant. A *pesante* theme (based on the chant "Christ Is Risen") enters in Piano I at the upbeat to measure 25 and continues through measure 30. Rachmaninoff was once offered some advice on the presentation of this theme. "At a performance of the work…Rimsky-Korsakov suggested that the chant would be appreciated more if it could be heard first without the bell imitation, an idea which Rachmaninov rejected immediately. In later years he realized the wisdom behind the suggestion."[4] After a breathtaking interlude, filled with sonorous *sf* chords in Piano I and brilliant octaves in Piano II, the chant theme returns at measure 39. The *accelerando* octave figuration and *ffff* chords at measures 53–58 conclude the *Fantaisie* gloriously.

The poem that precedes this movement is by Aleksey Stepanovich Khomyakov (1804–1860), a Russian theologian, poet, and artist. While few of his writings were published during his lifetime, they did later influence the Russian Orthodox Church.

Form (**ABABA Coda**):

Introduction = 1–2
A = 3–24
B = 25–30
A = 31–38
B = 38–44
A = 44–53
Coda = 53–58

---

3 Oskar von Riesemann, *Rachmaninoff's Recollections Told to Oskar von Riesemann* (New York: The MacMillan Company, 1934), 215–216.
4 John Culshaw, *Sergei Rachmaninov* (London: Dennis Dobson Limited, 1949), 30.

ABOUT THIS EDITION

This edition is based on the first edition published by Gutheil in 1893. Rachmaninoff included no fingering, pedal, or metronome markings.

Metronome markings and fingerings are editorial in this edition. Although no pedaling is included, the work requires tasteful pedaling by both performers. The pedal should be used throughout as needed without blurring the sound. Performers should adapt the pedaling to the acoustics of the room, the sonority of each piano (balanced with each other), and personal taste. All other editorial markings are in parentheses.

SOURCES CONSULTED

Bertensson, Sergei and Jay Leyda. *Sergei Rachmaninoff: A Lifetime in Music*. Bloomington, IN: Indiana University Press, 2001.

Culshaw, John. *Sergei Rachmaninov*. London: Dennis Dobson Limited, 1949.

Harrison, Max. *Rachmaninoff: Life, Works, Recordings*. London: Continuum, 2005.

Hinson, Maurice. *Music for More Than One Piano*. Bloomington, IN: Indiana University Press, 1988.

Martyn, Barrie. *Rachmaninoff: Composer, Pianist, Conductor*. Hants, England: Scholar Press, 1990.

Moldenhauer, Hans. *Duo-Pianism*. Chicago: Chicago Musical College Press, 1950.

Riesemann, Oskar von. *Rachmaninoff's Recollections Told to Oskar von Riesemann*. New York: The Macmillan Company, 1934.

Sadie, Stanley, ed. *The New Grove Dictionary of Music and Musicians*, Vol. 15. London: Macmillan Publishers Limited, 1980.

to Peter Ilyich Tchaikovsky

FANTAISIE-TABLEAUX
Suite No. 1
(1893)

I. Barcarolle

A cold evening wave
Is barely rustling under the oars of a gondola
. . . .
. . .it's day again, and again the guitar is singing!
. . . .
Afar is heard the sound of the barcarolle:
"The gondola's on the water gliding
And time on wings of love is flying;
The water will again regain its level,
But the passion will never be resurrected!"

Mikhail Yuryevich Lermontov (1814–1841)

Sergei Rachmaninoff (1873–1943)
Op. 5

(a) Begin the trill on D, the principal note. Notice that the E-flat changes to E-natural in measure 86.

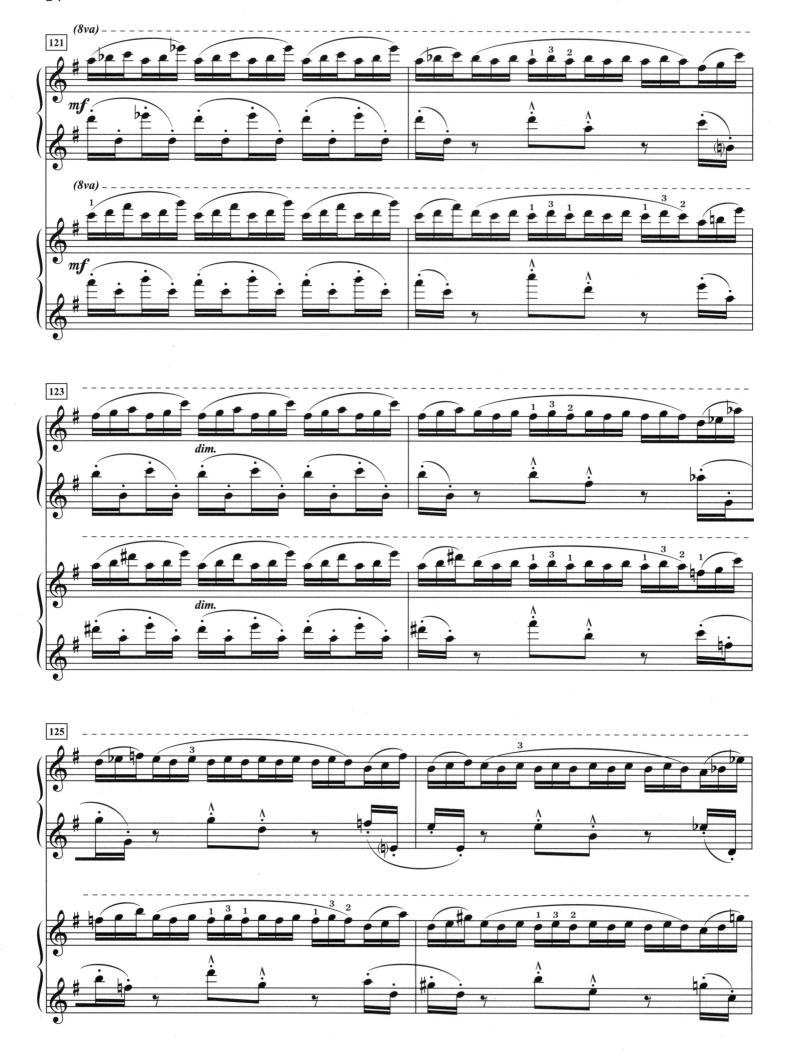

ⓑ Begin the trill on D, the principal note. Notice that the E-flat changes to E-natural in measure 130.

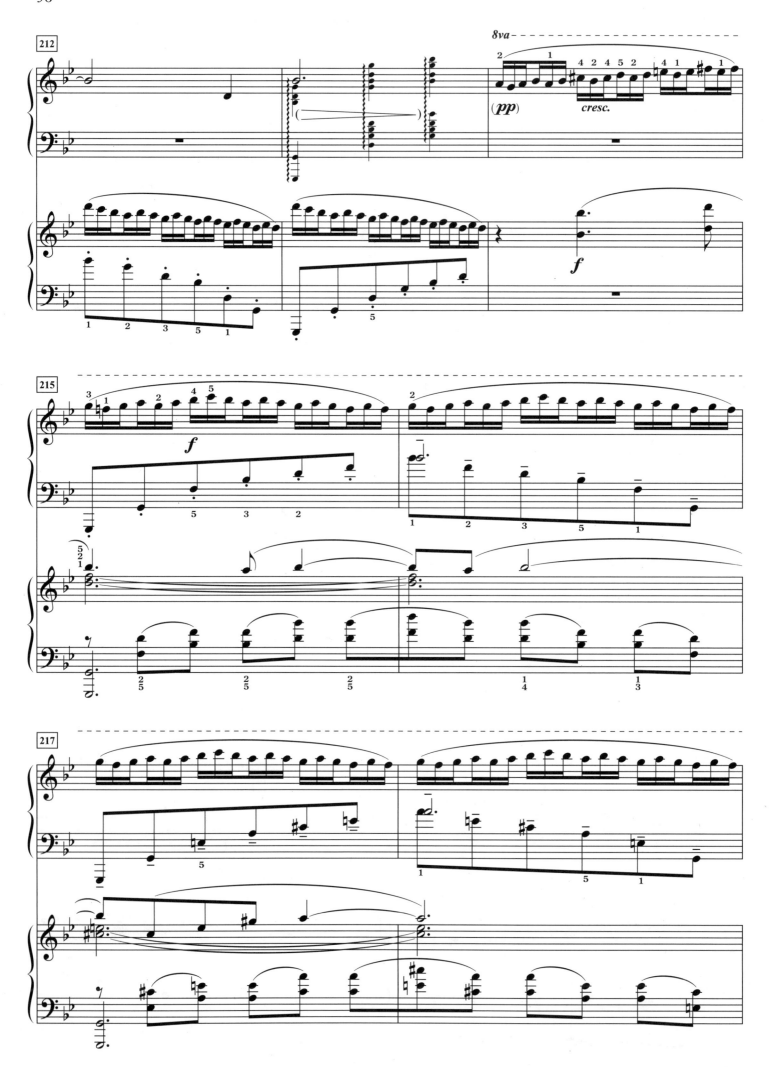

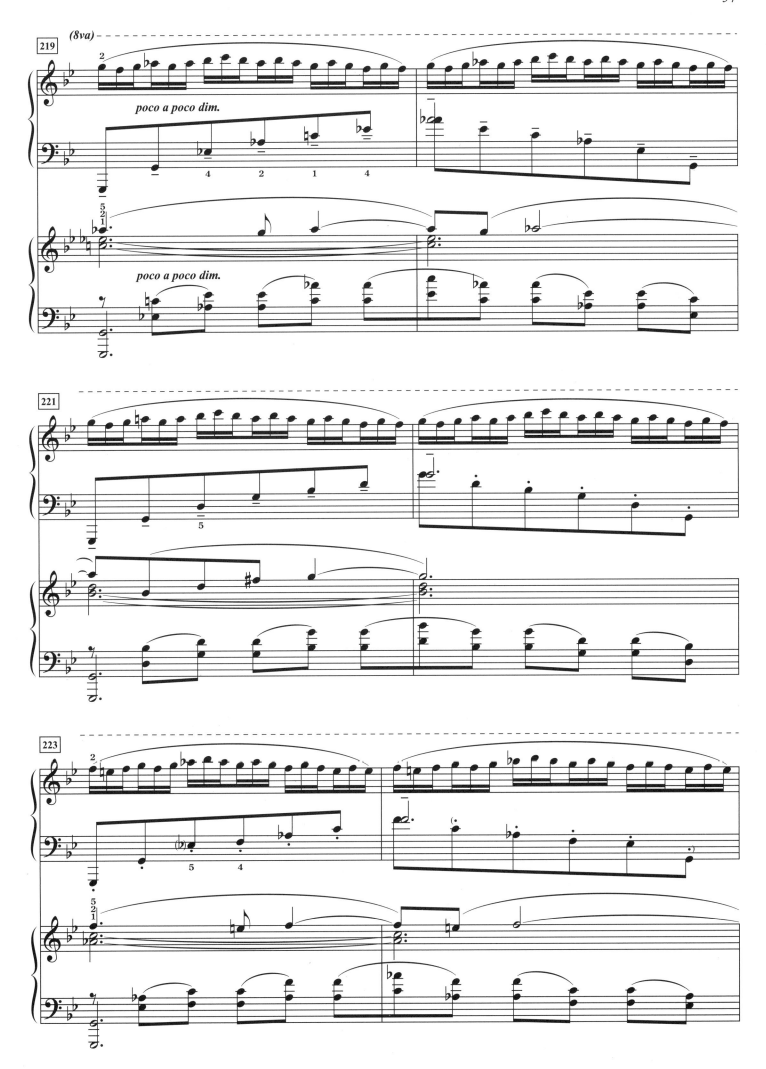

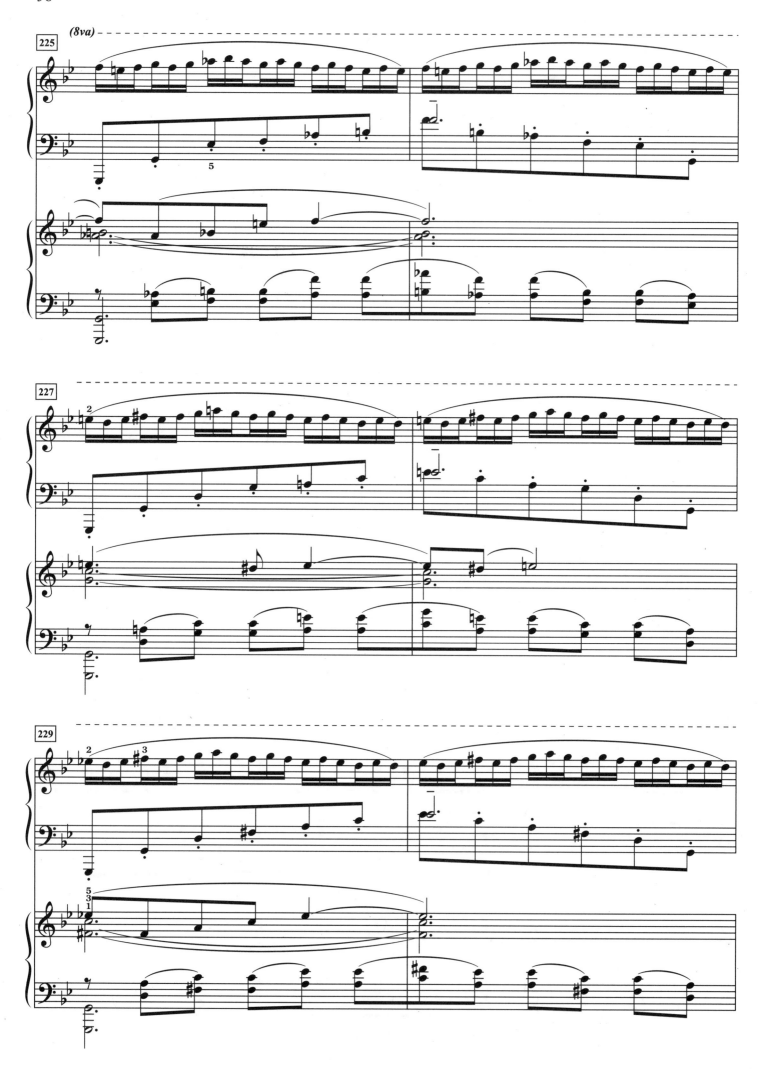

ⓒ Pianists with small hands may omit the lower B-flat in the RH of measures 234 and 238.

II. La nuit, l'amour
(A Night for Love)

It is the hour when from the boughs
The nightingale's high note is heard;
It is the hour when lover's vows
Seem sweet in every whispered word;
And gentle winds, and waters near,
Make music to the lonely ear.

George Gordon Byron (1788–1824)
(Lord Byron)

ⓐ Begin the trill on C, the principal note.

(b) Play the *acciaccatura*, the small grace note, very quickly before the principal note.

46

© Pianists with small hands may omit the B-natural in the RH.

ⓓ Pianists with small hands may omit the D in the RH.
ⓔ Piano I may use the sostenuto pedal in mm. 51–54 and 56–59.
ⓕ Play the bottom four notes on the beat quickly followed by the top note.

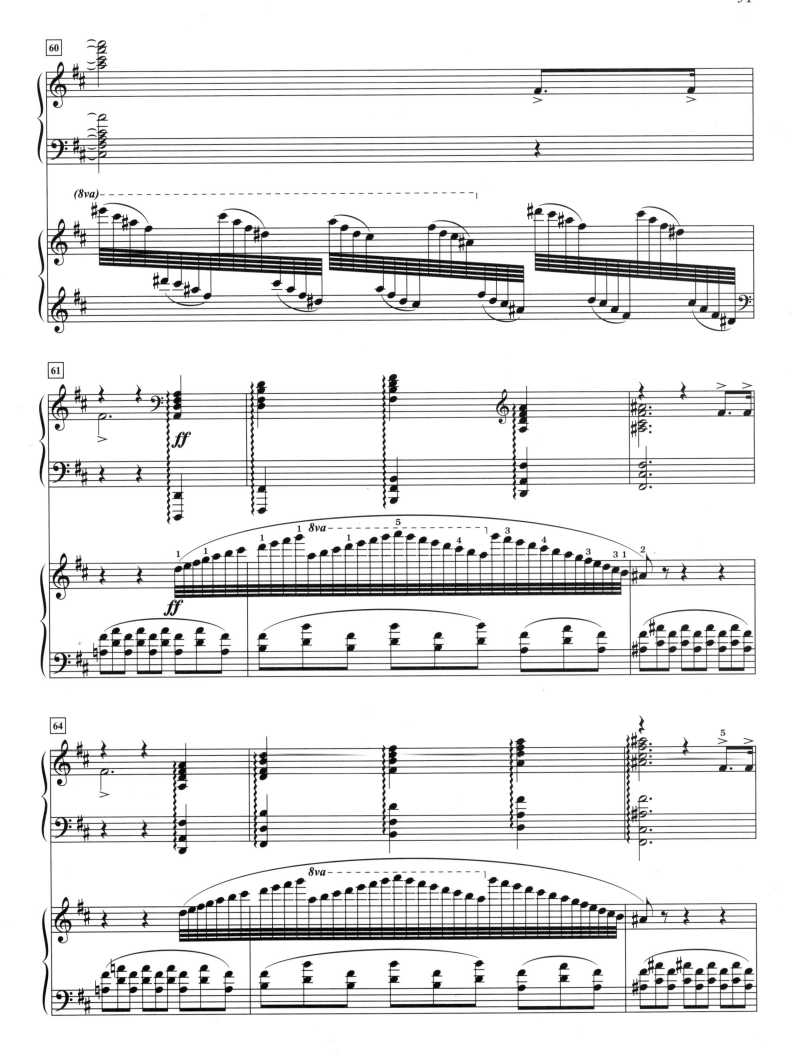

(g) Begin the small notes together on the beat and adjust the speed of the arpeggios
   so that the F-sharp dotted half notes are played together.

III. Les larmes
(Tears)

Human tears, oh human tears!
Flowing in early and late season—
Flowing unknown, flowing unseen,
Inexhaustible, as they may seem,
Flowing like rivers from the sky
On a bleak autumn night.

Fyodor Ivanovich Tyutchev (1803–1873)

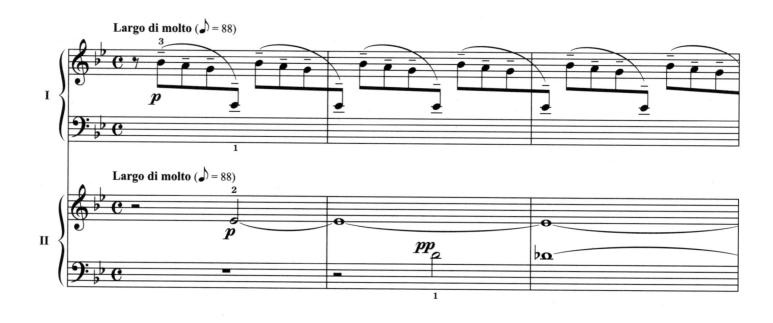

IV. Pâques
(Russian Easter)

And mighty chiming flew across the earth,
And the ringing air began to tremble,
The singing silver thunders
Proclaiming the news of holy celebrations.

Aleksey Stepanovich Khomyakov (1804–1860)